Cooking For Girls

imagine THAT!

Imagine That! is an imprint of Top That! Publishing plc,
Tide Mill Way, Woodbridge, Suffolk, IP12 IAP, UK
www.topthatpublishing.com
Copyright © 2009 Top That! Publishing plc
Imagine That! is a trademark of Top That! Publishing plc.

Contents

Cooking Equipment

Before you begin to get creative in the kitchen, it's a good idea to take a look through the drawers and cupboards to make sure you know where all the cooking equipment is kept.

• To complete the recipes in this book, you will need to use a selection of everyday cooking equipment and utensils, such as mixing bowls, saucepans, a sieve, knives, spoons and forks and a chopping board.

• Of course, you'll need to weigh and measure the ingredients, so you'll need a measuring jug and some kitchen scales too.

• Some of the recipes tell you to use a whisk. Ask an adult to help you use an electric whisk, or you can use a balloon whisk yourself – you'll just have to work extra hard!

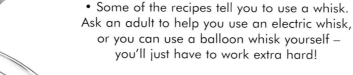

• To make some of the recipes in this book, you'll need to use the correct-sized tins or other special equipment. These items (and others that you may not have to hand) are listed at the start of each recipe.

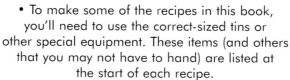

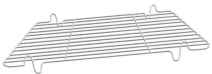

Safety and Hygiene

It is important to take care in the kitchen as there are lots of potential hazards and hygiene risks.

 Take Note! Whenever you see the warning triangle you will need adult supervision.

- Before starting any cooking always wash your hands.

- Cover any cuts with a plaster.

- Wear an apron to protect your clothes.

- Always make sure that all the equipment you use is clean.

- If you need to use a sharp knife to cut up something hard, ask an adult to help you. Always use a chopping board.

- Remember that trays in the oven and pans on the cooker can get very hot. Always ask an adult to turn on the oven and to get things in and out of the oven for you.

- Always ask an adult for help if you are using anything electrical – like an electric whisk.

- Be careful when heating anything in a pan on top of the cooker. Keep the handle turned to one side to avoid accidentally knocking the pan.

- Keep your pets out of the kitchen while cooking.

Getting Started

Making your own snacks, meals, cakes and drinks is great fun and really quite easy. Best of all, everyone will enjoy what you create!

Measuring:

Use scales to weigh exactly how much of each ingredient you need or use a measuring jug to measure liquids.

Mixing:

Use a spoon, balloon whisk or electric hand whisk to mix the ingredients together.

Different ideas:

Decorate your cakes and biscuits with flavoured or coloured icing, and then add chocolate drops, sweets or sugar strands. Experiment with the savoury recipes to find something you like.

Different shapes:

Cookie cutters come in lots of different shapes and sizes, and can be bought from most supermarkets. If you don't have any cookie cutters of your own, carefully use a knife to cut out the shapes you want.

Creating recipes:

Once you've made a recipe in this book a few times, think about whether you could make your own version. Why not mix some chocolate chips into the Yummy Flapjacks mixture or add mushrooms to the Cheese and Ham Toasties? This way you can start to make up your own recipes. Try to think up names for the things you create!

Read through each recipe to make sure you've got all the ingredients that you need before you start.

Always ask an adult for help if you are not sure about anything.

Light Snacks

Scrummy snacks for you to make and enjoy!

Cheesy Party Pockets

These cheesy pockets are perfect for any party!

Cheesy Party Pockets

1. Roll out the pastry so it is ½ cm (¼ in.) thick. Cut into 8 cm (3 in.) squares and brush the edges with beaten egg.

You will need:

Extra equipment:
pastry brush
rolling pin

Ingredients:
375 g (12 oz) puff pastry
1 egg yolk (beaten with
1 tablespoon water)
450 g (1 lb) favourite cheese
4 tablespoons fresh
parsley, chopped
freshly ground black pepper
3 teaspoons of sesame seeds

Preheat the oven to 200°C /
390°F / gas mark 6

Makes
20

2. Cut the cheese into 20 slices. Put a slice onto each piece of pastry, sprinkle with parsley, and season with black pepper.

3. Pinch together the corners of the pastry and flatten slightly. Place the pastry onto an oiled baking tray and brush with more beaten egg. Sprinkle with sesame seeds.

4. Bake for 15 minutes in the oven, until the pastry has puffed up. Serve warm or at room temperature.

Spicy Potato Wedges

A perfect snack! Why not dip the wedges into the homemade salsa on page 27?

Spicy Potato Wedges

1. Scrub the potatoes, but do not peel. Cut each potato in half and then each half into about five wedges. Put them into a large bowl.

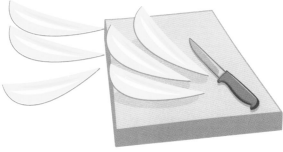

You will need:

Extra equipment:
Pestle and mortar or rolling pin

Ingredients:
5 medium potatoes
1 teaspoon coriander seeds
1 teaspoon cumin seeds
4-5 whole black peppercorns
4-5 tablespoons extra
virgin olive oil
a dash of chilli sauce

Preheat the oven to 200°C / 390°F / gas mark 6

Makes
50

2. Crush the coriander, cumin and peppercorns using a pestle and mortar, or using the end of a rolling pin.

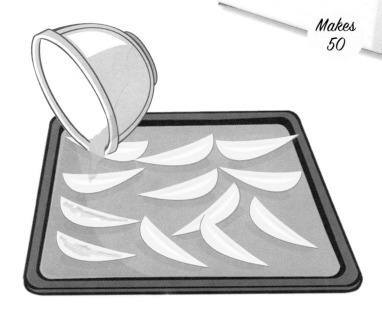

3. Mix the oil and chilli sauce with the crushed spices and pour over the potatoes, coating well.

4. Put the potatoes on a baking tray and bake in the oven for 25–30 minutes until cooked through. Stir the potatoes around during cooking to stop them burning.

Serve hot.

Sausage Rolls

These yummy sausage rolls won't stick around for long!

Sausage Rolls

1. Melt the butter in a saucepan and add the onions. Cook gently for about 20 minutes until soft and golden brown. Then, spread out on a plate to cool.

You will need:

Extra equipment:
a rolling pin
a pastry brush

Ingredients:
1 tablespoon butter
1 red onion, peeled and finely sliced
6 pork sausages
a handful of breadcrumbs
2 tablespoons plain flour
250 g (10 oz) ready-made puff pastry
1 egg
a little milk

Preheat the oven to 180°C / 355°F / gas mark 4

Makes
10

2. Ask an adult to slit the skins of the sausages and pop the meat out. Put the meat in a mixing bowl with the onion and the breadcrumbs, and then scrunch well, with clean hands, to mix together.

3. On a floured work surface, roll the pastry out into a rectangle so it is about 1 cm (½ in.) thick. Then, cut it lengthways into two long, even rectangles. Roll the mixture, made in step 2, into sausage shapes with your hands, and lay along the centre of each rectangle.

4. Mix the egg and milk and brush over the pastry. Then, fold one side of the pastry over the filling. Press down with your fingers or the edge of a spoon to seal.

5. Cut the long rolls into the size you want and space them out on a baking tray. Brush with the rest of the egg and bake for 25 minutes or until puffed and golden.

Mini Pizzas

If you like pizza, you'll love these delicious mini pizzas!

Mini Pizzas

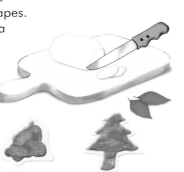

1. Empty the pizza base mix into a bowl, add the water, and mix, according to the packet instructions.

2. Using a rolling pin, roll the pizza mix dough so it is about 2 cm (1 in.) thick. Use the cookie cutters to cut out shapes. They can be a star, a Christmas tree or anything you like!

3. Next, spread the tomato purée onto the base. Then, add the mozzarella cheese and the herbs.

4. Add the topping of your choice. Why not add a few different toppings, such as brie and cranberry or perhaps a sweet topping like pineapple!

5. Ask an adult to place the mini pizzas into a pre-heated oven for 10–15 minutes or until they are piping hot and the bases are golden brown!

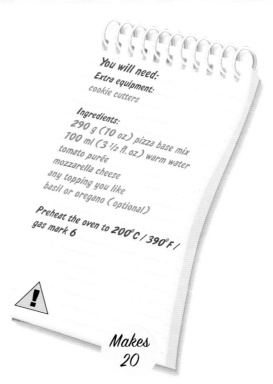

You will need:
Extra equipment:
cookie cutters

Ingredients:
290 g (10 oz) pizza base mix
100 ml (3 ½ fl. oz) warm water
tomato purée
mozzarella cheese
any topping you like
basil or oregano (optional)

Preheat the oven to 200°C / 390°F / gas mark 6

Makes 20

Puff Pastry Twists

These scrummy twists are great as an after-school snack!

Puff Pastry Twists

1. Ask an adult to cut 10 cm (4 in.) strips from the rolled puff pastry.

You will need:

Extra equipment:
Deep fat fryer or deep frying pan, if not using the oven method

Ingredients:
2 sheets ready-rolled puff pastry
2 tablespoons plain flour
1 beaten egg
sugar for dusting
vegetable oil for frying

Preheat the oven to 200°C / 390°F / gas mark 6

Makes 24

2. Put enough vegetable oil in a pan to cover the twists, or use a deep fat fryer. Ask an adult to heat the oil to 190°C (375°F), or until a piece of pastry dropped in the oil is sizzling and brown in thirty seconds.

3. Twist the puff pastry strips and ask an adult to drop them into the oil to cook. When puffed up and golden, ask an adult to remove from the oil, drain, and place on a paper towel. Dust liberally with sugar while still warm.

4. If you prefer, you can cook the pastry twists on a baking tray in the oven at 200°C (400°F). Brush with the beaten egg and cook for 5–10 minutes until golden brown and puffed. Put on a wire rack to cool and dust with sugar while still warm.

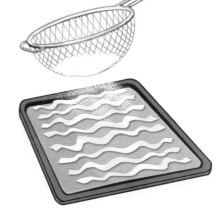

Fantastic Filo Parcels

Dig in to these parcels to release the gooey cheese centre!

Fantastic Filo Parcels

You will need:

Extra equipment:
pastry brush

Ingredients:
4 sheets of pre-made filo pastry
200 g (8 oz) brie
4 tablespoons of olive oil
4 heaped teaspoons of
cranberry sauce

Preheat the oven to 200°C / 390°F /
gas mark 6

1. Ask an adult to cut each piece of filo into four quarters and also to cut the brie into four.

2. To make a parcel, brush one of the pieces of filo pastry with olive oil. Put another piece over it to make a cross and brush with oil again. Lay a third piece diagonally, as if you were making a star shape, brush with oil, then top with the final piece, diagonally (see below), and brush with oil.

Makes
4

3. Place one of the pieces of brie in the centre of the pastry and put a heaped teaspoon of cranberry sauce on top of it. Fold up the sides of the filo and scrunch them at the top so they hold together. Brush all over with olive oil. Make three more parcels in the same way.

4. Place all of the parcels on a lightly oiled baking sheet and bake in the oven for 15–20 minutes, or until crisp and lightly browned.

Spicy Chicken Wings

These spicy chicken wings are too hot to handle!

Spicy Chicken Wings

1. First, make the marinade by combining all of the dry ingredients. Mix together well, then add the lemon juice and orange juice and stir.

2. Place the chicken wings in a deep bowl and cover with the spicy marinade. Cover and refrigerate for at least 6 hours.

3. Remove the wings from the marinade and place onto a baking tray. Return the marinade to a saucepan, and heat on a low setting until it has thickened.

4. Place the wings under the grill on a medium heat for about 20–25 minutes, turning occasionally and basting with the sauce.

You will need:

Ingredients:

1 teaspoon crushed red pepper
2 teaspoons cajun seasoning
1 teaspoon chilli powder
½ teaspoon cornflour
6 tablespoons brown sugar
100 ml (3 fl. oz) lemon juice
500 ml (17 fl. oz) orange juice
1 kg (2 lbs, 2 oz) chicken wings
1 tablespoon oil

Preheat the grill to a medium heat

Serves 4-6

Top Tip!

Be extra careful when handling raw chicken. Remember to thoroughly wash your hands, immediately after you touch it.

Veggie Dips and Hummus

This finger food will go down a treat at any sleepover!

Veggie Dips and Hummus

For the hummus:

1. Ask an adult to roast the red peppers in the oven until they are soft. Once they are cool, peel off the skins.

2. Place the red peppers and the rest of the hummus ingredients into a blender and blend until smooth.

You will need:
Extra equipment:
blender

Ingredients:
For the hummus:
2 red peppers, deseeded and cut into 4
400 g (14 oz) canned chickpeas
2 cloves of garlic
juice of ½ lemon
45 ml (3 tbsp) olive oil

A selection of fresh vegetables:
carrots
celery
cucumber
peppers

⚠

Serves 4

For the vegetables:

1. First, wash and prepare the vegetables.

2. Ask an adult to help you peel and chop up the vegetables into sticks.

3. Now, scoop the hummus into a small bowl and serve with your veggie dips!

Cheese and Ham Toasties

The melted cheese combined with the ham makes these toasties the ultimate tasty snack!

Cheese and Ham Toasties

1. Spread the butter onto one side of each of the slices of bread. Place one slice onto a preheated toastie maker, butter-side down, and layer the slices of cheese, ham and tomato, if using.

You will need:

Extra equipment:
sandwich toastie maker

Ingredients:
50 g (2 oz) butter
4 slices of bread, white or brown
100 g (4 oz) cheddar cheese, sliced
4 slices of ham
1 tomato, sliced (optional)

Makes 2

2. Place the other slice of bread on top to complete the sandwich, making sure the butter is facing upwards. (This is so the bread does not stick to the toastie maker.)

3. Close the lid and cook for 2–3 minutes, until the cheese has melted and the bread is golden brown.

Top Tip!
Try different fillings and see which one you like best!

Nachos and Tomato Salsa

Ideal for a light snack on summer evenings or as finger food at a party!

Nachos and Tomato Salsa

1. Ask an adult to chop the tomatoes into small pieces, making sure there are no seeds, and place into a bowl.

2. Place the remaining salsa ingredients into the bowl and mix together well before transferring into a small serving bowl.

You will need:
Extra equipment:
baking tray

Ingredients:
1 pack of tortilla crisps
50 g (2 oz) cheddar cheese, grated
1 jalapeno pepper, chopped (optional)

For the salsa:
350 g (12 oz) fresh tomatoes
½ red onion, chopped
1 tablespoon coriander, chopped
2 cloves garlic, peeled and crushed

Preheat the grill

⚠️

Serves
2

3. Scatter the tortilla crisps onto a baking tray and sprinkle the cheese and chopped jalapenoes over the top so the crisps are evenly covered.

5. Dip your nachos into the salsa and enjoy a taste sensation!

Top Tip!

Why not add some guacamole and sour cream to your nachos!

4. Place the baking tray under a preheated grill for 3–4 minutes, until the cheese has melted.

Main Meals

Impress your friends and family with these gorgeous main meals!

Pasta Carbonara

This creamy pasta dish is so delicious you'll want to make it again and again!

Pasta Carbonara

1. Heat the oil in a large pan over a medium heat. Add the onion and cook for 4–5 minutes until soft.

2. Add the bacon or pancetta and carry on cooking for another 7–8 minutes, stirring all the time.

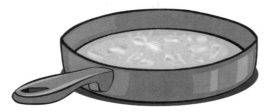

3. Meanwhile, cook the pasta in plenty of boiling, salted water until it is just cooked.

4. Lightly whisk the eggs and cream together in a bowl. Add 50 g (2 oz) of the Parmesan cheese and season with a little salt and plenty of black pepper.

5. Drain the pasta and tip into the pan with the onion and bacon. Turn off the heat and add the egg and cream mixture.

6. Toss everything together vigorously so that the egg cooks in the hot pasta.

7. Serve with extra black pepper and the rest of the Parmesan cheese.

You will need:

Ingredients:

2 tablespoons olive oil

1 small onion, finely chopped

200 g (7 oz) streaky bacon or pancetta, cut into cubes

350 g (12 oz) pasta

4 eggs

400 ml (14 fl. oz) double cream

75 g (3 oz) freshly grated Parmesan cheese

salt and black pepper

Serves 4–6

Veggie Stir-fry

Whip up a quick and healthy meal for your friends and family!

Veggie Stir-fry

1 Heat the oil in the wok, and fry the spring onions, garlic and ginger on a high heat.

2. Add the mange tout, baby corn, asparagus, pepper and mushrooms, and stir-fry for a minute or two.

3. Add the tomatoes and cook briskly to evaporate the excess liquid.

You will need:

Extra equipment:
wok

Ingredients:
1 tablespoon oil
4 spring onions, cut into 2 ½ cm (1 in.) lengths
4 garlic cloves, crushed
2 ½ cm (1 in.) ginger, chopped
100 g (4 oz) mange tout
100 g (4 oz) baby corn
100 g (4 oz) baby asparagus
1 red pepper, diced
100 g (4 oz) mushrooms, sliced
2 tomatoes, skinned, deseeded and chopped
1 tablespoon dark soy sauce
freshly ground black pepper

Serves
4

4. Add the soy sauce, taste, season with the black pepper and serve.

Great Greek Salad

Fantastic as an accompaniment to a main meal or on its own.

Great Greek Salad

1. Place the diced cucumber, tomatoes, olives, if using, and feta into a large bowl and mix together well.

2. Toss in the cos lettuce. Don't be afraid to use your hands – it's all part of the fun! (Remember to wash them first though!).

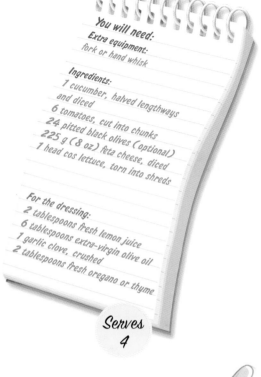

You will need:

Extra equipment:
fork or hand whisk

Ingredients:
1 cucumber, halved lengthways and diced
6 tomatoes, cut into chunks
24 pitted black olives (optional)
225 g (8 oz) feta cheese, diced
1 head cos lettuce, torn into shreds

For the dressing:
2 tablespoons fresh lemon juice
6 tablespoons extra-virgin olive oil
1 garlic clove, crushed
2 tablespoons fresh oregano or thyme

Serves
4

2. Whisk the dressing ingredients in a separate bowl with a fork. Then, drizzle over the Greek salad and serve.

Beef Burgers

Invite your friends over and wow them with these fab burgers!

Beef Burgers

1. Place the minced beef in a large bowl and add the remaining ingredients. Mix it all together, either with your hands or a spoon, until just combined.

You will need:
Ingredients:
1 kg (2 lb, 2 oz) minced beef
1 onion, finely chopped
4 tablespoons fine breadcrumbs
2 eggs, lightly beaten
salt and pepper to season
1 teaspoon mustard
2 cloves garlic, peeled and crushed

Serve with burger buns, salad and a slice of cheese or bacon

⚠ Preheat the grill / pan / barbecue to a medium heat

Makes
8

2. Wet your hands, and then mould the mixture into a burger shape about 2 cm (1 in.) thick.

4. Cook the burgers for about 5 minutes on each side, turning them once.

3. The burgers can now be cooked either on a griddle pan, non-stick frying pan with a bit of oil, or on a barbecue. Make sure you preheat the frying pan, griddle pan or barbecue to a medium heat before placing the burgers on top.

Top Tip!

Why not add some of the homemade tomato salsa to your burger (see recipe on p.27)

Easy Chicken Curry

This chicken curry is so good you'll be dishing out seconds!

Easy Chicken Curry

1. Heat the oil in a large saucepan and fry the chicken pieces, until browned.

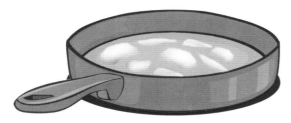

2. Next, add the pepper and onion to the pan and fry gently, until softened.

3. In a bowl, combine the tomatoes, coriander, paprika, ginger, salt, chilli, turmeric, cinnamon and cloves and finally stir in the chicken stock. Then, pour into the pan.

4. Cover and cook in a preheated oven for 2–3 hours.

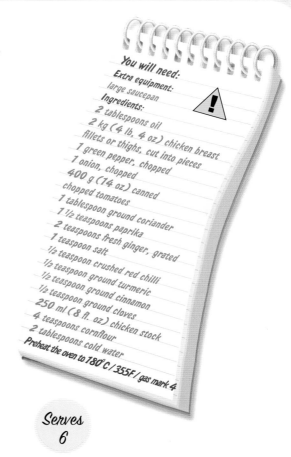

You will need:

Extra equipment:
large saucepan

Ingredients:
2 tablespoons oil
2 kg (4 lb, 4 oz) chicken breast fillets or thighs, cut into pieces
1 green pepper, chopped
1 onion, chopped
400 g (14 oz) canned chopped tomatoes
1 tablespoon ground coriander
1 ½ teaspoons paprika
2 teaspoons fresh ginger, grated
1 teaspoon salt
½ teaspoon crushed red chilli
½ teaspoon ground turmeric
½ teaspoon ground cinnamon
½ teaspoon ground cloves
250 ml (8 fl. oz) chicken stock
4 teaspoons cornflour
2 tablespoons cold water
Preheat the oven to 180°C / 355F / gas mark 4

Serves
6

5. In the last thirty minutes of cooking time, combine the cornflour and cold water in a bowl, and then stir into the pan. Cover and cook for a further 15–20 minutes, or until the sauce has thickened.

Serve with pilau rice and naan bread.

Sausage Casserole

This wholesome sausage casserole is a great winter-warmer!

Sausage Casserole

1. Heat the oil in a saucepan on a medium heat. Add the sausages and gently brown them.

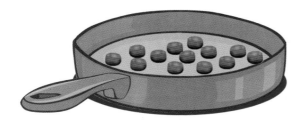

2. Next, add the onion and fry for 2 minutes. Then, place the rest of the ingredients into the saucepan, except for the cornflour.

3. Cover the saucepan with a lid and cook in a preheated oven for 2–3 hours.

4. When ready to serve, mix a couple of tablespoons of cornflour with some water in a bowl, then pour the mixture into the casserole. Simmer on the stove until the sauce is the required thickness.

Serve with fresh, crusty bread or with mashed potatoes and vegetables.

You will need:
Extra equipment:
large saucepan
Ingredients:
1 tablespoon oil
8 good-quality sausages, cut into chunks
1 medium onion, diced
150 g (5 oz) whole baby carrots
3 large potatoes, cut into pieces
400 g (14 oz) canned kidney beans, drained
100 g (4 oz) green beans
150 g (5 oz) button mushrooms
500 ml (17 fl. oz) chicken stock
squirt of tomato purée
150 ml (5 fl. oz) red wine
2 bay leaves
cornflour to thicken
Preheat the oven to 180C / 355F / gas mark 4

Serves
4

Variation:

Try this recipe with different flavoured sausages! For example, if you like spicy food, add Mexican sausages, adding chilli to the casserole. Whatever sausage you choose, try to adapt the recipe to complement the flavour of the sausage.

Fabulous Fishcakes

These yummy fishcakes are fab for any occasion!

Fabulous Fishcakes

1. Drain the salmon and put into a bowl. Mash with a fork, removing any large bones. Add the mashed potato, followed by the rest of the ingredients.

2. Dust your hands with flour and form the mixture into 12–15 cakes.

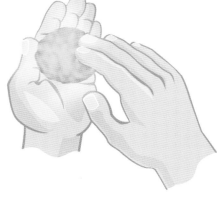

3. Coat each cake in flour, then dip into the beaten egg and finally into the breadcrumbs. Set aside in the fridge for at least one hour so the fishcakes can set.

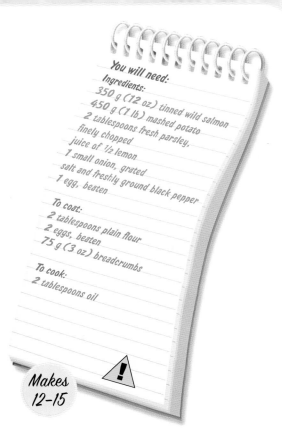

You will need:

Ingredients:
350 g (12 oz) tinned wild salmon
450 g (1 lb) mashed potato
2 tablespoons fresh parsley, finely chopped
juice of ½ lemon
1 small onion, grated
salt and freshly ground black pepper
1 egg, beaten

To coat:
2 tablespoons plain flour
2 eggs, beaten
75 g (3 oz) breadcrumbs

To cook:
2 tablespoons oil

Makes
12–15

4. Heat 2 tablespoons of oil in a deep frying pan and cook the fishcakes over a medium heat, a few at a time, for 2–3 minutes on each side until golden brown and crisp.

Serve with a fresh salad and a slice of lemon!

Sweet Treats

Mmm ... make and taste these mouth-watering sweet treats!

Chocolate Truffles

A box of these chocolate truffles makes the perfect present!

Chocolate Truffles

1. Ask an adult to put a heatproof bowl over a saucepan of just-simmering water. Make sure the bowl doesn't touch the water. Break the chocolate into small pieces and put them into the bowl, and then add the cream and butter. Stir the mixture until the chocolate has melted.

You will need:
Extra equipment:
paper sweet cases
a plastic container

Ingredients:
200 g (7 oz) plain chocolate
200 ml (7 fl. oz) double cream
25 g (1 oz) butter

To coat the truffles:
cocoa powder
chocolate strands
desiccated coconut

⚠️

Makes
20

2. Take the saucepan off the heat. Take the bowl off the saucepan and leave it to cool for a few minutes. Carefully pour the melted chocolate into the container. Put the lid on the container and leave it in the fridge to set for 3–4 hours.

4. Roll the balls in cocoa powder, and then put them into the paper cases. Store the truffles in a container in the fridge until you're ready to eat them or give them as a gift.

3. Remove the container from the fridge. Roll small balls of the chocolate mixture in your hands.

Top Tip!
You'll have to roll the truffle balls quickly or the mixture will literally melt in your hands! Why not roll the truffles in chocolate strands or desiccated coconut?

Coconut Ice

These simple sweets can be made in any colours you like!

Coconut Ice

1. Put the tin on the greaseproof paper, and draw around it. Cut out the square so that it is large enough to overlap the sides. Then, slit the corners and put it into the tin.

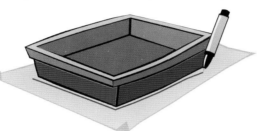

You will need:
Extra equipment:
a square baking tin 18 cm (7 in.)
greaseproof baking paper

Ingredients:
225 g (8 oz) icing sugar
25 g (1 oz) butter
150 ml (5 fl.oz) sweetened condensed milk
225 g (8 oz) desiccated coconut
food colouring

Makes 30

2. Ask an adult to help you put the sugar, butter and sweetened condensed milk into a pan over a medium heat, and bring the mixture to the boil. Let the mixture simmer for four minutes, stirring all the time.

5. Colour the other half of the mixture with a few drops of food colouring. Pour it on top of the mixture in the tin, and leave it to set. Cut the Coconut Ice into squares, but be careful – it will be very crumbly!

3. Remove the pan from the heat and stir in the coconut.

4. Ask an adult to pour half of the mixture into the tin. Leave it to cool.

Chocolate Fudge

A wonderful treat for anyone who loves chocolate!

Chocolate Fudge

1. Line the tin with greaseproof paper. Ask an adult to help you put the chocolate and the condensed milk into a saucepan over a medium heat. Stir them together until the chocolate has melted.

You will need:
Extra equipment:
a square baking tin 15 cm (6 in.)
an icing syringe
paper sweet cases
greaseproof paper

Ingredients:
300 g (10 oz) plain chocolate
200 ml (7 fl oz) sweetened
condensed milk

Makes
20-24

2. Ask an adult to pour the mixture into the tin, and smooth the top with the back of a spoon. Put the tin into the fridge for 3–4 hours.

3. Remove the fudge from the tin by lifting it with the baking paper. Turn it out onto a board and peel off the paper.

Cut the slab of fudge into squares and serve!

Top Tip!

Add white or dark chocolate to make different flavoured fudge!

Peppermint Creams

An icy cool kick for you and your friends!

Peppermint Creams

1. Sift the icing sugar into a bowl.

2. Whisk the egg white in a bowl until it's frothy, then add it to the icing sugar with a few drops of peppermint essence. Mix it together with the wooden spoon to make a very thick paste. Knead the paste with your hands until it is very smooth.

You will need:
Ingredients:
450 g (1 lb) icing sugar
1 egg white
a few drops of peppermint essence
food colouring (optional)

For chocolate peppermint creams:
100 g (4 oz) plain chocolate, melted

Makes 30-40

3. To make coloured peppermint creams, put some of the mixture into another bowl and add one or two drops of food colouring. Mix it well. Do this for every different colour used.

4. Use your hands to make small balls of paste and flatten them into discs. Put them onto a wire rack to harden slightly.

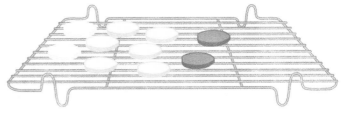

5. You could dip your peppermint creams into melted chocolate. Leave them to set on the wire rack.

Fruity Ice Lollies

These gorgeous ice lollies will keep you cool on any hot summer day!

Fruity Ice Lollies

1. Place the fruit, yogurt and sugar into a blender and blend until smooth. (If you have not got a blender, place the ingredients into a bowl and ask an adult to blend the mixture with a hand-held electric whisk.)

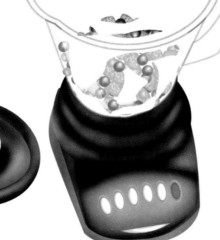

You will need:
Extra equipment:
ice lolly moulds
blender

Ingredients:
200 g (7 oz) of your favourite fruit
e.g blackcurrants, strawberries etc
225 ml (8 fl oz) natural yogurt or
good quality fruit yogurt
3 tablespoons powdered sugar

Makes 8-10

2. Tip the mixture into a jug, and then pour into the lolly moulds. Put the moulds into a freezer and let them set for at least 4 hours, until solid.

Top Tip!
Any leftover fruit can be used to make a smoothie! Just mix it in a blender with some yogurt and milk!

Jewel Jellies

These wobbling jellies will liven up any party!

Jewel Jellies

1. Place the jelly into a heatproof measuring jug and pour over 300 ml (10 fl. oz) of boiling water. Stir with a spoon until the jelly has dissolved.

2. Stir the fruit into the jug.

3. Pour the mixture into six individual jelly moulds or into one big mould. Place into the fridge to set for at least 3 hours.

You will need:
Extra equipment:
jelly moulds
heatproof jug

Ingredients:
135 g (5 oz) pack of flavoured jelly
150 g (5 ½ oz) mixed frozen
berries / fruit
300 ml (10 fl. oz) boiling water

⚠️

Serves
6

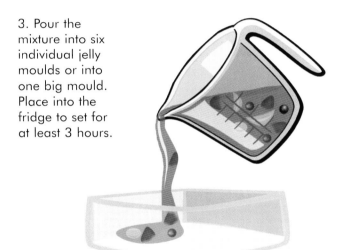

5. Gently shake until the jelly loosens onto the plate.

4. To unmould the jellies so they are ready to serve, ask an adult to half fill a bowl with hot water. Dip the jelly moulds, one at a time, briefly in the water, and then lift out and quicky place the serving plate over the top.

Decorate with extra berries for a pretty finish and serve with ice cream!

Fab Fruit Kebabs

Choose your favourite fruits to make colourful fruity kebabs!

Fab Fruit Kebabs

1. Wash and prepare the fruit to start with.
Cut the strawberries in half and cut the mango,
orange, pineapple etc. into thick slices.

You will need:
Extra equipment:
Skewers

Ingredients:
A selection of fresh fruits:
8 strawberries
8 seedless grapes
8 pieces of kiwi
8 pieces of orange
8 pieces of mango
8 pieces of banana
8 pieces of pineapple

Makes
4

2. Push the fruit onto the skewers, alternating
the different types of fruit.

Top Tip!

Try this with lots of different fruits.
Which combinations work best together?
Drizzle with strawberry sauce (see page 59)
for a girly flourish!

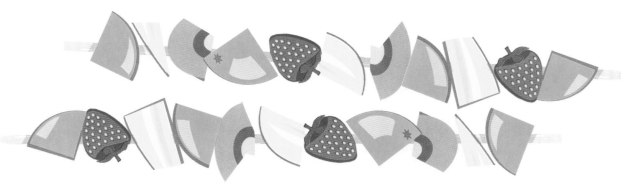

Strawberry Cheesecake

This heavenly cheesecake is easy to make and simply scrumptious!

Strawberry Cheesecake

1. Butter and line a 23 cm (9 in.) loose-bottomed tin with baking parchment. Then, put the biscuits in a plastic food bag and crush using a rolling pin.

2. Transfer the crumbs to a bowl, then pour over the melted butter. Mix thoroughly until the crumbs are completely coated.

3. Tip them into the prepared tin and press firmly down into the base to create an even layer. Chill in the fridge for 1 hour to set firmly.

4. Ask an adult to prepare the vanilla pod, by scraping out the seeds using the back of a knife.

5. Next, place the soft cheese, 100 g (4 oz) of icing sugar and vanilla seeds in a bowl, then ask an adult to beat with an electric mixer until smooth. Tip in the cream and continue beating until the mixture is completely combined. Next, spoon the mixture onto the biscuit base. Smooth the top of the cheesecake down with the back of a spatula and leave to set in the fridge overnight.

You will need:

Extra equipment:
23 cm (9 in.) loose-bottomed tin
baking parchment
plastic food bag
rolling pin
electric mixer and blender

Ingredients:
250 g (9 oz) digestive biscuits
100 g (4 oz) butter, melted
1 vanilla pod
600 g (21 oz) soft cheese
100 g (4 oz) icing sugar
250 ml (10 fl. oz) double cream
100 g (4 oz) strawberries, hulled and sliced
2 teaspoons water

Serves 12

6. To serve, place the base on top of a serving plate, then gradually pull the sides of the tin down, removing the lining paper and base.

7. Ask an adult to purée the strawberries in a blender with 50 g (2 oz) of icing sugar and 2 teaspoons of water, then sieve. Swirl the purée onto the cake with a knife.

Baking

Create, bake and decorate a range of delicious delights!

Chocolate Chip Muffins

These yummy chocolate chip muffins are great for parties!

Chocolate Chip Muffins

1. Use a paper towel to grease the muffin tray with a little soft butter.

You will need:
Extra equipment:
a muffin baking tray

Ingredients:
150 g (5 oz.) butter
150 g (5 oz.) brown sugar
2 eggs
150 g (5 oz.) self-raising flour
1 tablespoon cocoa powder
75-100 ml (3-4 fl. oz.) milk
75 g (3 oz) chocolate chips

Preheat the oven to 180°C / 355°F / gas mark 4

Makes
12

2. Put the butter, sugar and eggs into a large mixing bowl. Sift in the flour. Stir the ingredients together with a wooden spoon until well mixed.

3. Sift the cocoa powder into the bowl. Add the milk until the mixture is creamy and add the chocolate chips. Mix them together.

4. Use a teaspoon to divide the mixture equally into the muffin tray. Bake the muffins for 12 minutes.

5. Leave the muffins in the tray until they are cool, and then decorate them with icing if you want to (see page 65 for the ingredients and method).

Top Tip!

To soften the butter, take it out of the fridge at least 30 minutes before cooking.

Magical Muffins

Use lots of brightly coloured icing to decorate these brilliant cakes!

Magical Muffins

1. Put the paper cases in the muffin baking tray.

You will need:
Extra equipment:
paper cases
a muffin baking tray
an icing syringe (optional)

Ingredients:
100 g (4 oz) self-raising flour
100 g (4 oz) margarine
100 g (4 oz) caster sugar
2 eggs
75-100 ml (3-4 fl. oz) milk

To decorate:
for water icing:
100 g (4 oz)
icing sugar
1-2 tablespoons
of water
food colouring

for royal icing:
100 g (4 oz)
icing sugar
1 egg white
food colouring

Preheat the oven to 200°C /
390°F / gas mark 6

Makes
10-12

2. Sift the flour into a bowl. Add the margarine. Use the tips of your fingers to rub the margarine and flour together until the mixture becomes crumbly.

3. Add the sugar and mix it in. Now stir in the egg. Finally, add enough milk to make the mixture creamy.

4. Put spoonfuls of the mixture into the paper cases. Bake the muffins for 10–15 minutes, until they are golden brown. Leave them to cool on a wire rack.

Decorating the Muffins

1. Cover the muffins with water icing. Here's how to make it! Sift the icing sugar into a bowl. Add 1–2 tablespoons of hot water and mix until you have a smooth thick paste. Add one or two drops of food colouring if you want coloured icing.

To make chocolate icing, add one teaspoon of cocoa powder to the icing sugar before sifting. To make lemon icing, add 1–2 tablespoons of lemon juice instead of hot water.

You can decorate your muffins with sugar sprinkles, silver balls or sweets. Once the water icing has set, why not add some more decorations with royal icing?

2. To make royal icing, beat an egg white in a small bowl. Sift the icing sugar into the bowl. Beat the mixture until the icing becomes smooth and thick. Add a drop of food colouring if you wish. Spoon the icing into an icing syringe

and carefully pipe your decoration onto the muffins. Leave the icing to set.

Top Tip!

Decorate your muffins with sugared diamonds, sugar sprinkles, silver balls or small sweets!

Variations:

White Chocolate Chip Muffins
Sift 25 g (1 oz) cocoa into the bowl with the flour. Mix in a handful of white chocolate chips. When the muffins are cooked and cooled, cover them with chocolate water icing (see method above).

Coconut Muffins
Add 50 g (2 oz) desiccated coconut to the mixture with the sugar. When the muffins are cooked, top them with lemon water icing (see method above) and sprinkle them with more coconut.

Cherry Muffins
Add 100 g (4 oz) chopped glacé cherries to the mixture with the sugar. When the muffins are cooked, cover them with lemon water icing (see method above) and top each muffin with half a glacé cherry.

Caramel Cupcakes

Sticky caramel and chocolate ... yummy!

Caramel Cupcakes

1. Put the paper cases in the bun tin.

You will need:
Extra equipment:
a bun tin and paper cases

Ingredients:
100 g (4 oz) dark chocolate
145 g (5 oz) butter
145 g (5 oz) brown sugar
80 g (3 oz) golden syrup
155 ml (5 fl oz) milk
125 g (4 ½ oz) plain flour
40 g (2 oz) self-raising flour
1 egg – lightly beaten

For the topping:
150 g (5 oz) butter – softened
250 g (9 oz) icing sugar
2 tablespoons cocoa powder
2 teaspoons hot water
chopped nuts and chocolate chips

Preheat the oven to 180°C / 355°F /
gas mark 4

Makes
12

2. Place the chocolate, butter, sugar, syrup and milk in a small saucepan. Stir over a low heat until melted and smooth. Leave to cool for about 15 minutes.

3. Sift the plain flour and self-raising flour into a bowl.

4. Add the flour into the caramel mixture. Next stir in the egg and mix until just combined.

5. Use a teaspoon to transfer equal amounts of the mixture to the paper cases. Bake the cupcakes for about 20 minutes. Leave them to cool on a wire rack.

6. For the topping, beat together the butter and icing sugar. Combine the cocoa powder with the water, and add to the mixture. Beat until smooth and creamy. Swirl over the cupcakes, adding a few chopped nuts and chocolate chips if you like.

Crackle Cakes

Use cornflakes or crisped rice to make these little cakes crackle!

Crackle Cakes

1. Put the sugar, butter, cocoa powder and golden syrup or honey into a pan over a low heat. Stir until the ingredients have melted.

You will need:
Extra equipment:
paper sweet cases

Ingredients:
50 g (2 oz) sugar
50 g (2 oz) butter
3 tablespoons cocoa powder
2 tablespoons golden syrup or honey
50 g (2 oz) cornflakes

To decorate:
coloured chocolate drops

Makes 8-10

2. Stir the cornflakes into the mixture until they are completely coated.

3. Spoon a little of the mixture into each of the paper cases. Top each with a coloured chocolate drop and leave them to set.

Top Tip!
Use crisped rice instead of cornflakes if you prefer.

Gingerbread Men

Create your own gingerbread family with this great recipe!

Gingerbread Men

1. Use a paper towel to grease the baking tray with a little margarine. Sift the flour, bicarbonate of soda, ground ginger and ground cinnamon into a mixing bowl.

2. Rub in the butter with your fingertips until it looks like breadcrumbs. Next, add the sugar.

3. In a separate saucepan or bowl, mix together the egg and golden syrup and then add to the dry ingredients. Mix together until it forms a dough.

4. Put the dough onto a floured surface and, and gently roll it out (not too thinly) with a rolling pin. Cut out shapes, putting them onto a baking tray as you go. Collect the dough trimmings into a ball and roll them out to make more biscuits. Bake in the oven for 10–15 minutes. Cool on a wire rack.

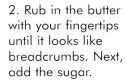

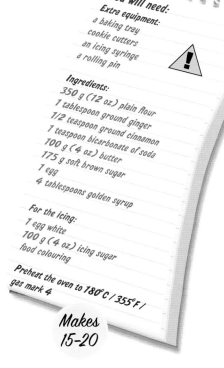

You will need:
Extra equipment:
a baking tray
cookie cutters
an icing syringe
a rolling pin

Ingredients:
350 g (12 oz) plain flour
1 tablespoon ground ginger
1/2 teaspoon ground cinnamon
1 teaspoon bicarbonate of soda
100 g (4 oz) butter
175 g soft brown sugar
1 egg
4 tablespoons golden syrup

For the icing:
1 egg white
100 g (4 oz) icing sugar
food colouring

Preheat the oven to 180°C / 355°F / gas mark 4

Makes 15-20

5. To make the icing, beat the egg white in a small bowl, and then sift the icing sugar on top. Beat the ingredients together until you have a smooth, stiff paste, and add a few drops of food colouring if you like. Spoon the icing into a syringe and decorate your gingerbread men!

Butterfly Buns

These buns may look fancy, but they're simple to make!

Butterfly Buns

1. Put the paper cases in the bun tray.

You will need:
Extra equipment:
a bun tray
paper cases

Ingredients:
100 g (4 oz) butter
100 g (4 oz) granulated sugar
2 eggs
100 g (4 oz) self-raising flour

For the buttercream icing:
75 g (3 oz) butter
150 g (6 oz) icing sugar
1-2 tablespoons milk
food colouring (optional)

Preheat the oven to 190°C /
375°F / gas mark 5

2. Put the butter and sugar into a mixing bowl. Use a wooden spoon to beat them together until the mixture is fluffy and very pale in colour.

Makes
10-12

3. Beat in the eggs, one at a time, adding a tablespoon of flour with each one.

4. Sift the rest of the flour into the bowl. Use a tablespoon to mix the ingredients gently, as if you were drawing a figure-of-eight. This will make sure your mixture stays nice and fluffy.

5. Use a teaspoon to transfer equal amounts of the mixture to the bun cases. Bake the buns for 10–15 minutes or until they are well risen and golden brown. Leave them to cool on a wire rack.

6. To make the butterfly wings, cut a slice from the top of each cake. Now cut each slice in half. Place a little royal icing on top of each bun (see page 65) and then gently push the wings on top of each cake.

Yummy Flapjacks

These yummy flapjacks are packed with oats!

Yummy Flapjacks

1. Use a paper towel to grease the tin with a little butter. Put the butter, sugar and honey (or golden syrup) in a pan over a low heat. Stir the ingredients together until the butter has melted and the sugar has dissolved.

You will need:
Extra equipment:
a baking tin 28 x 18 cm (11 x 7 in.)

Ingredients:
225 g (8 oz) butter
75 g (3 oz) sugar
2 tablespoons honey or golden syrup
350 g (12 oz) porridge oats

For fruit and nut flapjacks:
100 g (4 oz) sultanas, raisins or currants
50 g (2 oz) chopped nuts

For chocolate flapjacks:
100 g (4 oz) plain chocolate

Preheat the oven to 180°C / 350°F / gas mark 4

2. Take the pan off the heat and stir in the porridge oats, mixing well. If you are making fruit and nut flapjacks, stir these ingredients in as well.

Makes 12–15

3. Spread the mixture into the tin, and press it down with the back of a spoon. Bake the flapjacks for 20–25 minutes. Take care not to overcook them or they will taste too dry. Cut the mixture into twelve pieces, and leave them in the tin to cool completely.

Chocolate Flapjacks

1. Ask an adult to help you melt the chocolate in a heatproof bowl over a pan of simmering water (or use a microwave).

2. Take the bowl off the pan. Dip the ends of each flapjack into the melted chocolate, and leave them to set on a wire rack.

Summer Garden Cupcakes

Inspired by a beautiful garden in bloom!

Summer Garden Cupcakes

1. Put the paper cases in the bun tin.

2. Crack the eggs into a bowl and beat lightly with a fork.

3. Place the butter, sugar, flour and vanilla into a large bowl. Add the beaten egg and a couple of drops of green food colouring.

You will need:

Extra equipment:
a bun tin and paper cases

Ingredients:
3 eggs
150 g (5 oz) butter – softened
150 g (5 oz) sugar
175 g (6 oz) self-raising flour
1 teaspoon vanilla essence
2 drops green food colouring

For the topping:
150 g (5 oz) butter – softened
250 g (8 oz) icing sugar
1 teaspoon vanilla essence
2 teaspoons hot water
2 drops of green food colouring

Preheat the oven to 190°C / 375°F / gas mark 5

⚠️

Makes
12–15

4. Beat with an electric mixer for 2 minutes, until the mixture is light and creamy.

5. Use a teaspoon to transfer equal amounts of the mixture to the paper cases. Bake the cupcakes for 18–20 minutes. Leave them to cool on a wire rack.

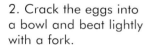

6. For the topping, beat together the butter and icing sugar. Once well mixed, add the vanilla, food colouring and water. Beat until smooth and creamy. Swirl over your cupcakes and decorate with flowers. If you use real flowers, remove them before eating!

Take Note!

Ask an adult to help you use the electric whisk.

Delightful Drinks

Treat your taste buds to these delightful drinks!

Strawberry Smoothie

This frothy concoction tastes as good as it looks!

Strawberry Smoothie

1. Place all of the ingredients into a blender and ask an adult to whizz until smooth.

2. Pour into two glasses.

3. Serve immediately.

Top Tip!
Decorate the glass with fruit and add a straw!

You will need:
Extra equipment:
blender

Ingredients:
3 handfuls strawberries, hulled and sliced
300 ml (10 fl. oz) creamy strawberry yogurt
4 ice cubes, crushed

Serves
2

Witches' Brew Smoothie

Trick or treaters will love this mint milkshake drink on Halloween!

Witches' Brew Smoothie

1. Place all of the ingredients into a blender and ask an adult to whizz until smooth.

You will need:
Extra equipment:
blender

Ingredients:
300 ml (10 fl. oz) milk
4 scoops mint ice cream
2 drops green food colouring

Serves
2

2. Pour into two glasses.

3. Serve immediately.

Top Tip!
Decorate with 'bats' eyeballs' (redcurrants or blackcurrants).

Fairy Froth Smoothie

This sweet and sparkly ice cream soda is perfect for parties with a pink theme!

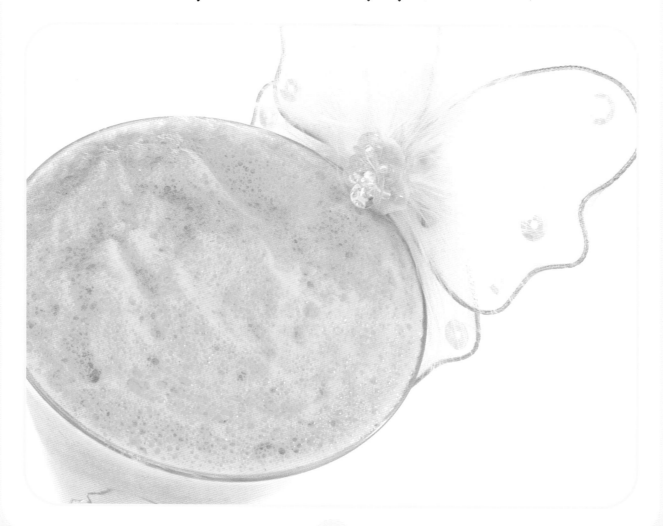

Fairy Froth Smoothie

1. Place all of the ingredients into a blender and ask an adult to whizz until smooth.

You will need:
Extra equipment:
blender

Ingredients:
300 ml (10 fl. oz) cherry soda
4 scoops vanilla ice cream

Serves
2

2. Pour into two glasses.

3. Serve immediately.

Top Tip!
Drizzle strawberry syrup over the top like a fairy necklace, and make sure there are enough magic wands to go round.

Cheeky Monkey Smoothie

This peanut butter and banana concoction is delicious!

Cheeky Monkey Smoothie

1. Place all of the ingredients into a blender and ask an adult to whizz until smooth.

You will need:
Extra equipment:
blender

Ingredients:
300 ml (10 fl.oz.) milk
dash chocolate syrup
1 generous tablespoon peanut butter
1 banana, sliced
3 scoops vanilla ice cream

Serves
2

2. Pour into two glasses.

3. Serve immediately.

Warning!
Contains
nuts.

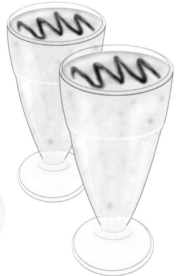

Summer Pudding Smoothie

This blended version is just as delicious as a real summer pudding!

Summer Pudding Smoothie

1. Place all of the ingredients into a blender and ask an adult to whizz until smooth.

You will need:
Extra equipment:
blender

Ingredients:
2 handfuls summer fruits
(redcurrants, blackcurrants,
raspberries)
150 ml (5 fl. oz) double cream
1 scoop vanilla ice cream

Serves
2

2. Pour into two glasses.

3. Serve immediately.

Top Tip!
Decorate with a scattering of blackcurrants.

Hot Chocolate

Cuddle up on a cold winter night with this gorgeous hot chocolate!

Hot Chocolate

1. Ask an adult to pour the milk into a pan and gently heat it along with the vanilla pod.

You will need:
Ingredients:
500 ml (17 fl. oz) full milk
1 vanilla pod
250 g (9 oz) chocolate, broken into pieces

⚠️

Serves 2

2. Add the chocolate pieces.

3. Bring the mixture to the boil, stirring frequently.

4. Remove the vanilla pod and serve.

Your Recipes

Use these pages to write down your own made-up recipes!

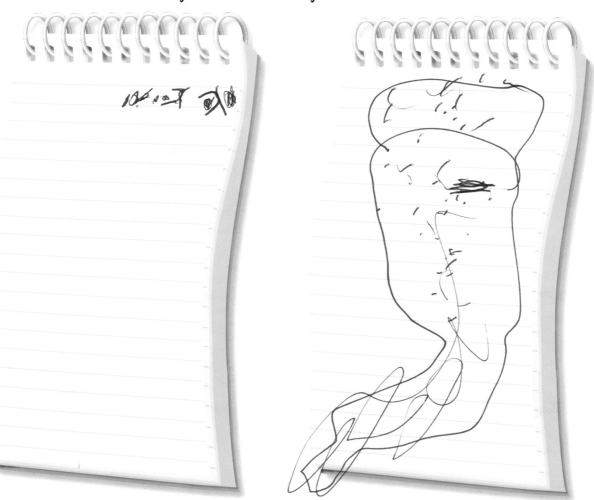

Your Recipes

Your Recipes

Your Recipes

Your Recipes